HOW TO DREAM

THICH NHAT HANH

PARALLAX
PRESS

BERKELEY, CALIFORNIA

Parallax Press
PO Box 7355
Berkeley, CA 94707
parallax.org

Parallax Press is the publishing division of Plum Village
Community of Engaged Buddhism, Inc.
© 2025 Plum Village Community of Engaged Buddhism
All rights reserved

Illustrations copyright © 2025 by Jason DeAntonis
Text design by Debbie Berne
Cover design by Katie Eberle
Typesetting by Maureen Forys, Happenstance Type-O-Rama

Printed in Canada by Friesens on FSC-certified paper

Parallax Press's authorized representative in the EEA is
SARL Boutique La Bambouseraie Point UH, Le Pey, 24240
Thénac, France. Email: europe@parallax.org

ISBN 978-1-952692-99-4
Ebook ISBN 978-0-938077-89-3

Library of Congress Control Number: 2025937384

1 2 3 4 5 FRIESENS 29 28 27 26 25

CONTENTS

NOTES ON DREAMING

A FIRE IN YOUR HEART

What is our greatest hope and aspiration if not a dream? Each moment of our daily lives, our dreams *can* slowly become reality.

Only faith, aspiration, awakening—only a big dream—can generate a collective energy powerful enough to bring our society to the shore of safety and hope. I know there is fire in your heart. Allow your dreams to carry you far and break free from the walls that limit you.

THE DEEPEST KIND OF DESIRE

A deep desire, or aspiration, is necessary for us to live. The Buddha had a name for this kind of desire: volition. A person's life is motivated by volition; it is the deepest kind of desire that we have in ourselves.

A BALL OF ENERGY

Volition is the driving motivation behind our thinking, speech, and actions. It determines everything. Every one of us has a strong goal for our life. We want to achieve something. We feel a ball of energy in us, a tremendous, powerful source of energy. We want to feel truly alive.

THE BUDDHA'S DEEPEST DESIRE

Before Siddhartha became the historical Buddha, he undertook six years of practice to become a free person, enlightened and emancipated. He had witnessed much suffering in his family, his society, and his country. He left his family and his position as a prince in his father's kingdom, but he was motivated by love, not by a desire to run away from his responsibilities. Siddhartha wanted to uproot the suffering in himself in order to offer others a way out. This was his deepest desire, and it brought him tremendous happiness. It gave him the courage and strength to go through many hardships.

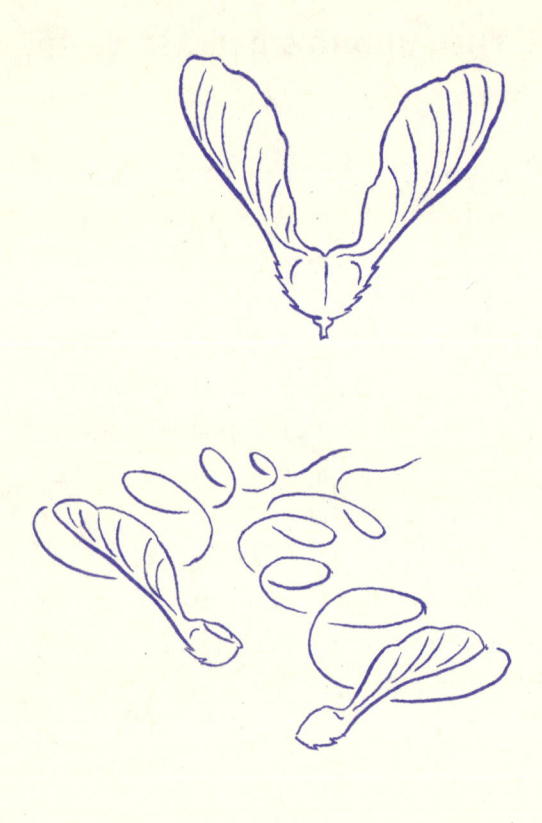

THE BUDDHA SEED

One day, when I was small, I saw a drawing
of the Buddha on the cover of a magazine.
The Buddha was sitting very peacefully on
the grass, his face was very calm, and he was
smiling. I was very impressed. Just looking at
the drawing made me happy, because so many
people around me at the time were not very
calm or happy at all.

Seeing this peaceful image, the idea came
to me that I wanted to become someone like
that Buddha, someone who could sit very still
and calm. I think that was the moment when
I first wanted to become a monk, although I
didn't know how to describe it that way at the
time. It is the first time the Buddha seed was
watered in me.

TAKE A CLOSER LOOK

Our volition can be nourishing, wholesome, and healthy, but there are kinds of volition which are unhealthy. Many whom we call terrorists have a strong desire to punish, kill, and get revenge, and that is also a kind of volition. That deep desire gives them a lot of energy, and they may even sacrifice their own lives for it. We need to examine our volition, our source of energy, to determine if it is wholesome or not.

THE POWER OF
UNWHOLESOME VOLITION

To illustrate the tragic power of our volition, the Buddha used the example of a young man who's being dragged toward a pit of fire by two strong men. The man wants to live; he's being dragged against his will. But the two men are stronger than he is, and they intend to throw him into the pit of fire. He doesn't want to die, but he can't resist. The Buddha asked, "Who are these two strong men who try to bring you to the realm of hell? They are your volition, your desire to run after what you believe to be happiness, namely the objects of your craving: craving for fame, craving for power, craving for sex, craving for wealth."

THE BEST KIND OF DREAM

We must look deeply into our volition to find out whether it is wholesome or unwholesome. If you find that your deepest desire is for fame, money, and sex, that desire can bring you a lot of suffering. If you are motivated by a desire to transform yourself and your community, to bring joy and hope into others' life, to be a powerful instrument for social change, then you have the best kind of volition. Such volition gives you an infinite source of energy, and you become very alive, full of vitality in your daily life.

TO BE HAPPY

To be happy, we need to take some time each day to sit down, look into ourselves, and identify the kind of energy that's motivating us and where it is pushing us. Are we being pushed in the direction of suffering and despair? If so, we must release this intention and find a more wholesome source of energy. Our volition should be *bodhicitta*, the mind of love, the intention to love and serve.

BODHICITTA: THE GREAT ASPIRATION

Bodhicitta is a Sanskrit term that means "the mind of awakening." It is sometimes called "the great aspiration." Our mind of awakening, or mind of love, is the deep wish to cultivate understanding in ourselves in order to bring happiness to many beings. It is the motivating force for the practice of mindful living.

TRANSFORMATION OCCURS RIGHT AWAY

Bodhicitta, our mind of love, is a tremendous source of power and energy; it can make us more alive. The seed of bodhicitta may have been buried in us for many years, under layers of suffering, sorrow, and forgetfulness. It needs to be touched, and when it is, transformation occurs right away. The moment we get in touch with our bodhicitta, people will see joy, energy, and hope in us, and everything we do or say will manifest its presence.

DREAMS BECOMING REAL

Bodhicitta is a reality, a living energy giving us faith and hope. Each moment of our daily lives, our dreams can slowly become reality. Over the past few decades, in my own life, I can tell you there's not a single moment when I haven't witnessed my dreams becoming real.

WHAT DO I WANT WITH MY LIFE?

The Buddha taught us to sit down, breathe, and look deeply into the question, "What is my deepest desire? Is it to have a lot of money, fame, sex, or something else? What do I want to do with my life?"

SITTING WITH WHAT'S ALIVE IN US

Sitting meditation is a way for us to return home to ourselves. Every time we sit down, whether it is in our living room, at the foot of a tree, or on a meditation cushion, we bring our full attention to what's happening in the present moment. Breathing and smiling with awareness, we let our mind become spacious and our heart soft and kind. The purpose of sitting is to be here, fully present with what's alive within and around us.

EXPERIENCING MINDFULNESS

Mindfulness is the energy of being aware and awake in the present moment. When we are mindful, we are paying attention, but to what? Mindfulness is always mindfulness of *something*. It always has an object.

Awareness of the breath is the essence of mindfulness. When we sit, we can become aware of our in-breath and out-breath. Follow your breath from the beginning of each inhale all the way through the end of each exhale. This is mindfulness of breathing. Each time we practice mindful breathing, we know a little more what mindfulness feels like.

MINDFULNESS MAKES US WHOLE

As soon as we pay attention to our breathing, body, breath, and mind come together. This can happen in just one or two seconds. You come back to yourself. Your awareness brings these three elements together, and you become fully present in the here and now. You are taking care of your body, you are taking care of your breath, and you are taking care of your mind.

When you make a soup, you have to add together all the right ingredients in harmony and let them simmer. Our breath is the broth that brings the different elements together. We bathe spirit and mind in our breath, and they become integrated so they are one thing. We are whole.

MINDFULNESS: THE HEART OF OUR DEEPEST DREAM

Our dream of togetherness, of deep compassion for ourselves and others, is possible right here and now. Mindfulness is at the heart of this awakening. We practice breathing to be able to be here in the present moment so that we can recognize what is happening in us and around us.

THREE VITAL ENERGIES

If you maintain the energy of mindfulness when you bring your attention to something, you'll naturally become concentrated on the object of your attention. Mindfulness and concentration are of the same essential nature, like water and ice.

When your mindfulness and concentration are powerful enough, you begin to have insight. Insight is enlightenment, understanding. We don't have to practice for a certain number of years in order to have insight; whenever there is mindfulness, there is already some insight.

A mindful in-breath contains insight. Aware that you're breathing in, you realize that you are alive; if you were not alive, you would not be breathing in. To be alive is a great miracle, and recognizing this, you can rejoice; your in-breath can be a celebration of being alive. Breathing mindfully and looking deeply like this, we can see the true nature of things.

TAKING ACTION IN OUR OWN LIVES

We may have a great desire to live in peace and to live sustainably, but most of us don't yet have concrete ways to act on that desire in our daily lives. We haven't yet organized ourselves. We haven't formed sustainable communities. We can't only blame our governments and corporations for the chemicals that pollute our drinking water, for the violence in our neighborhoods, or for the wars that destroy so many lives. It's time for each of us to wake up and take action in our own lives.

A CONCRETE PATH

Mindfulness is the continuous practice of touching deeply every moment of daily life. To be mindful is to be truly present with your body and your mind, to bring harmony to your intentions and actions, and to be in harmony with those around you.

We don't need to make a separate time for this outside of our daily activities. We can practice mindfulness in every moment of the day, in the kitchen, in the restroom, in our bedroom, and as we're going from one place to another. We can carry mindfulness with us as we wash the dishes, take a morning shower, or drive the car. We can do the same things we always do—walking, sitting, working, eating, and so on—with awareness of what we're doing. When we're eating, we know that we're eating. When we open a door, we know that we're opening the door.

The energy of mindfulness enables us to look deeply and gain the insight we need so that transformation—personal and societal—is possible.

CHANGING OUR CONSCIOUSNESS TO CHANGE THE WORLD

Consciousness is at the base of transformation. If we are not capable of changing our way of thinking, our way of perceiving, then any kind of action, no matter how direct, will not bring the kind of result we want. Sit-ins, teach-ins, and pray-ins are meaningful only when they are born from inner freedom, compassion, and understanding. If you have the wisdom of nondiscrimination, if you have the energy of understanding and compassion, then these kinds of actions can bring about real results. Social change follows directly from a change in our consciousness.

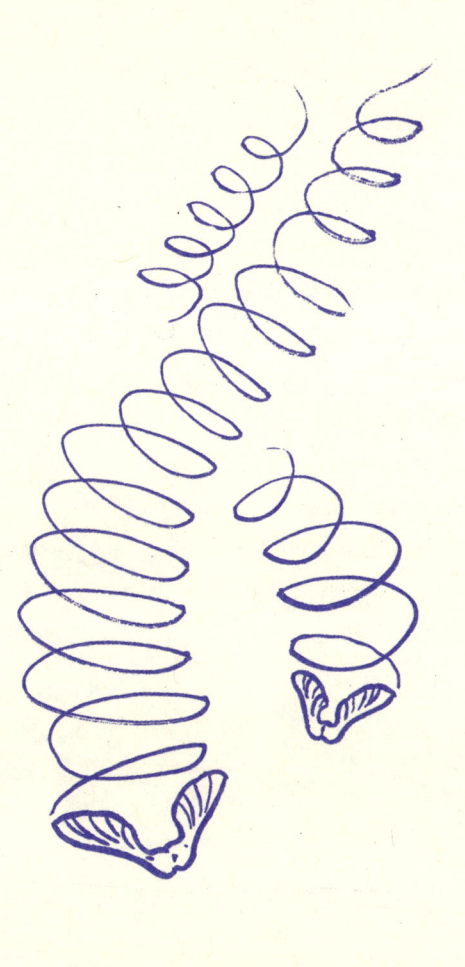

THE WISDOM OF NONDISCRIMINATION

With mindfulness and concentration, we can develop the wisdom of nondiscrimination and use it to guide our daily life. My right hand has written hundreds of poems. It can also write calligraphy and invite the bell. Yet it is not proud of itself. It never tells my left hand, "You are good for nothing. You don't write poems or practice calligraphy." Why? Because my right hand has the wisdom of nondiscrimination. It knows that it is also my left hand, and it acts according to that wisdom.

AS ONE

One day, as I held a nail in place with my left hand, my right hand, holding the hammer, missed the nail and pounded my finger instead. The moment my right hand made the mistake and caused me pain, it put down the hammer and started taking care of my left hand. My right hand did not say, "I am taking care of you, left hand. You should remember this." Likewise, my left hand did not say, "Right hand, you hurt me. Give me that hammer. I want revenge!" Each hand considered itself one with the other hand.

We need to look at each other in the same way as the right and left hands. If we act according to the spirit of nondiscrimination, we can bring about true peace.

A DREAM WE CAN REALIZE

Our dream must be one we can realize.
We cannot exploit and deplete our natural
resources for the sake of economic develop-
ment while also wishing to protect the environment. We cannot wish for peace at home while
exploiting the labor forces of other countries.
We must learn to live more simply: to live
simply yet happily, without overconsuming.

A PROMISING SIGN

I know many young people who prefer to work less, perhaps four hours a day, earning a small livelihood, so they can live simply and happily. This may be a solution to our society's problems—reducing the production of useless goods, sharing work with those who have none, and living simply and happily. Some individuals and communities have already proved that it's possible. This is a promising sign for the future, isn't it?

EXPRESSING OUR COMPASSION

Right Livelihood is the kind of occupation
that will not cause suffering, and allows us to
express our ideal of compassion and understanding. Those of us who have the kind of job
that can help us express our love, our care, and
our compassion should be happy about that.
It's wonderful to have that kind of livelihood.
Even if it brings less money, it brings much
happiness.

WORKING GENTLY

In my community, I used to bind books. Using a toothbrush, a small wheel, and a very heavy fireproof brick, I could bind two hundred books in a day. I was at peace while assembling the pages, gluing them, and putting the cover on the book. I knew I could not produce as many books in a day as a professional bookbinder or a machine, but I also knew that I didn't hate my job. If you want a lot of money to spend, you must work hard and quickly, but if you live simply, you can work gently with full awareness.

LIVING SIMPLY AND HAPPILY

Many people have shown it is possible to live simply yet happily. In our Plum Village community, no one has a private bank account, a personal cell phone, or individual plans for the future, and yet we are very happy. We have togetherness; we have opportunities every day to generate joy for ourselves and others and to live a dream that with each passing day becomes more of a reality. We learn to live deeply, to touch the wonders of life, and to recognize the treasure trove of joys available in the present moment.

A MOMENT OF LIFE

According to the Buddha, life is only available in the here and now. The past is already gone, and the future is yet to come. There is only one moment for me to live—the present moment.

By coming back to the present moment, I am able to touch life deeply. I can see the blue sky and hear the sound of the birds. My in-breath is life; my out-breath is life. Each step I take is life. If we can return to the here and now, we will be able to touch the many wonders of life that are available.

HAVING TIME

Your time is, first of all, for you to be: to be alive, to be peace, to be joy, and to be loving. The world needs joyous and loving people who are capable of just being without doing. If you know the art of being peace, of being solid, then you have the ground for every action.

RICH IN ASPIRATION

True happiness is grounded in freedom. We can live very simple lives and be happy, rich in aspiration and love. We must not be carried away by work or busyness so much that we don't have time to enjoy life. We should not look for happiness in shopping and consumption; we should find happiness in freedom. Being free, we have time to be in touch with the wonders of life within and around us.

AGENTS OF LIBERATION

We need freedom, but freedom from what? We need freedom from our sorrow and regret concerning the past. The past may have become a prison we can't escape from. Mindfulness helps us get out of the prison of the past and to be here now with the present moment.

The future can also be a prison. Many of us are afraid, uncertain, and anxious about the future. We have to get out of that prison. Breathing in, bringing the mind home to the body, and coming back to the present moment is already liberation. The energies of mindfulness, concentration, and insight are agents of liberation; they can help us to be free. True happiness is not possible without freedom.

NOT A MEANS TO AN END

Walking meditation is one way of waking up to the wonderful moment we are living in. If our mind is caught, distracted, or preoccupied with our worries and our suffering, we can't practice mindfulness; we can't enjoy the present moment, and we're missing out on life. But if we're awake, then we'll see this is a wonderful moment that life has given us, the only moment in which life is available. Walking meditation is not a means to an end. We can value each step we take, and each step can bring us happiness because we're in touch with life.

WALKING THE PATH OF PRACTICE TOGETHER

Our dream is to change the global situation we are living in, to help people come together to discuss their deepest concerns, their difficulties, their aspirations. There is a way out, and when we have a path of practice, we are no longer afraid. We need only to take our time and walk this path together.

BE THE CHANGE

Gandhi once said, "You must be the change you want to see in the world." If we know how to live a simpler, more relaxed, and happier life, our planet will have a future, and all species on our planet will have a future. This is a dream that we can realize today.

BECOMING A HERO TAKES TIME

Most of us are willing to spend six or eight years to get a diploma. We believe the diploma is necessary for our happiness. But very few of us are willing to spend three or six months or even a year to train ourselves to handle our sadness or our anger, to listen with compassion, and to use loving speech.

If you are able to transform your anger, sadness, and despair, if you are able to use loving speech and deep listening, you can become a hero capable of offering happiness to so many people.

TRANSFORMING DESPAIR

Our strong emotions are like a small child crying out for its mother. When a baby cries, the mother takes it gently in her arms and listens and observes carefully to find out what is wrong. The loving action of holding her baby with tenderness already soothes the baby's suffering. Likewise, we can take our strong emotions in our loving arms, and right away we will feel relief. We don't need to reject or suppress them. They are a part of us that need our love and deep listening just as a baby does. After the baby has calmed down, the mother can feel if the baby has a fever or needs a change of diaper. When we feel calm and cool, we too can look deeply at our strong emotions and see clearly the conditions that allowed them to arise.

MAKING PEACE POSSIBLE

Deep listening simply means listening with compassion. Even if the other person's words are full of wrong perceptions, discrimination, blame, and judgment, you can sit quietly and listen, without reaction or interruption. You know that if you can listen like that, the other person will feel enormous relief. You are listening with only one purpose in mind: to give the other person a chance to express themselves. It may be true that, up until now, no one has taken the time to listen. This is a practice of compassion.

Loving speech is another important aspect of practice. It is the kind of speech that inspires others. We only need to choose our words carefully, and we can make other people very happy. With loving speech, we speak the truth, but in a way that others can understand and accept. The way we speak can offer others joy, happiness, self-confidence, hope, trust, and insight.

If we use deep listening and loving speech, communication will be possible. Once communication is restored, peace also becomes possible.

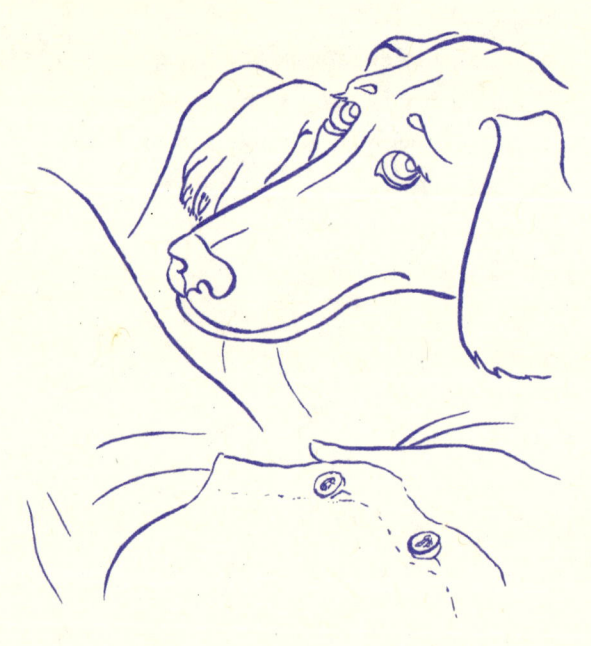

CONVEYING OUR DREAMS

We can begin by practicing mindful communication with those closest to us. Then when we speak to our larger community, people will listen because we embody love, peace, and compassion. We have already done our own inner work, and we practice what we preach. With the practice of loving speech and deep listening, we can convey our hopes and dreams to others and offer a path forward.

PEACE IS WITH YOU IMMEDIATELY

During a particularly difficult moment in my life,* I practiced with the phrase "If you want peace, peace is with you immediately." I was surprised to find myself quite calm, not afraid or worried about anything. I was not just being careless. This was truly a peaceful state of mind, and in that state, I was able to overcome this difficult situation.

---

* In 1976, Thich Nhat Hanh and several others were conducting an operation to rescue boat people in the Gulf of Siam. After they were exposed by the press, the Singaporean authorities arrived in the middle of the night to seize Thich Nhat Hanh's travel documents and order him to leave the country within twenty-four hours. This meant that, in twenty-four hours, 800 people on two boats would be stranded without food and water, unable to be brought ashore. In the hours that followed the police visit, Thich Nhat Hanh practiced mindful breathing, sitting, and walking. With a peaceful mind, he developed a plan for his visa to be extended by the French embassy. Just before the authorities' deadline, his visa was extended for a few days, giving him enough time to bring the boat people to relative safety.

As long as I live, I will never forget those moments of sitting meditation, those breaths, those mindful steps during that night and that morning. I vowed that if I could not have peace at that moment, I would never be able to have peace. If I could not be peaceful amid danger, the kind of peace I might realize in easier times would not mean anything. Practicing with "If you want peace, peace is with you immediately," I was able to resolve many problems, one after another.

ALWAYS ANOTHER "THIS"

Peace can exist only in the present moment. It is ridiculous to say, "Wait until I finish this, then I will be free to live in peace." What is "this"? A diploma, a job, a house, the payment of a debt? If you think that way, peace will never come. There is always another "this" that will follow the present one. If you are not living in peace at this moment, you will never be able to. If you truly want to be at peace, you must be at peace right now. Otherwise, there is only the hope of peace "someday."

HOPE CAN BE AN OBSTACLE

We all know that hope is necessary for life. But according to Buddhism, hope can be an obstacle. If we invest our mind in the future, we will not have enough mental energy to face and transform the present. Naturally, we have the right to make plans for the future, but that does not mean being swept away by daydreams. While we are making plans, our feet are firmly planted in the present. We can only build the future from the raw materials of the present.

AN IMPORTANT WISH

Peace does not come only after many long days of practice. What is most important is your wish, your deep aspiration, and your determination. If your determination is strong, the effect will follow the cause more quickly than a bolt of lightning.

PEACE MAKES US INDESTRUCTIBLE

The peace we seek cannot be our personal possession. We need to find an inner peace which makes it possible for us to become one with those who suffer and to do something to help them.

Real peace is not a barricade that separates you from the world. On the contrary, this kind of peace brings you into the world and empowers you to change society, to sow seeds of understanding, reconciliation, and compassion.

In any struggle, you need determination and patience, but this determination will dissipate if you lack peace. Those who lead a life of social action especially need to practice peace in each moment of daily life.

Our strength is in our peace, the peace within us. This peace makes us indestructible.

PEACE IS THE WAY

There is no way to peace: peace is the way.
The process that gives rise to peace must also
be peace. Dropping bombs and shooting guns
in the name of peace cannot work because
if the means are violent, the ends will also
be violent. Every word, every thought, every
action should contain peace within it if we are
on the path of peace.

ON THE RIGHT PATH

Happiness means feeling you are on the right path every moment. You don't need to arrive at the end of the path in order to be happy. The right path refers to the very concrete ways you live your life.

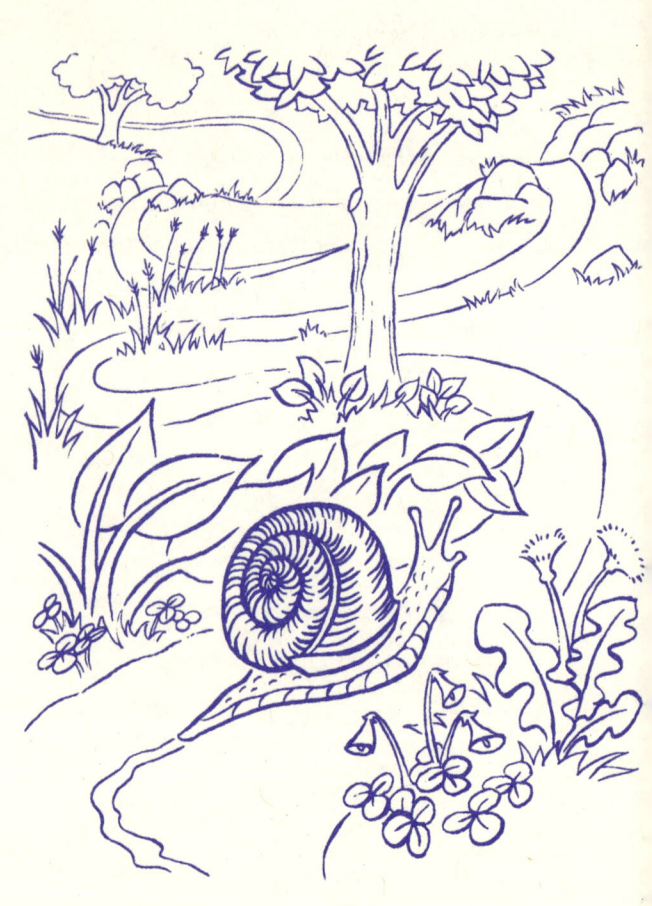

CHARTING A
DIFFERENT COURSE

Every day we do things, we *are* things that
contribute to peace. If we are aware of our life-
style, our way of consuming, our way of seeing
things, we will know how to make peace right
in the present moment. If we are very aware,
we can do something to change the course
of history.

MAKE GOOD CHOICES

Mindful consumption is not only about what we eat and drink. What we hear, see, feel, and think are also foods we consume through our senses, and what we read, watch, and listen to doesn't need to cause more suffering for ourselves and others.

We must learn what to consume and what not to consume in order to keep our bodies, our minds, and the earth healthy. Mindful consumption is the way out of our difficulties—not just our personal difficulties but also the way out of war, poverty, and climate crisis. The earth needs us to consume mindfully if we are to survive and thrive as a species.

WE NEED A BIGGER DREAM

For most of us who want to have a house, a car, a refrigerator, a television, and so on, we must sacrifice our time and our lives in exchange. We are constantly under the pressure of time. We have constructed a system we can't control. It imposes itself on us, and we become its slaves and victims. We need a kind of collective awakening.

"ASK THE HORSE!"

There is a story in Zen circles about a man and a horse. The horse is galloping quickly, and it appears that the man on the horse is going somewhere important. Another man, standing alongside the road, shouts, "Where are you going?" The first man replies, "I don't know! Ask the horse!"

This is also our story. We are riding a horse, we don't know where we are going, and we can't stop. The horse is our habit energy pulling us along, and we are powerless. We are always running, and it has become a habit. We struggle all the time, even while we sleep. We need to stop our horse and reclaim our liberty.

DON'T RUN

We are always trying to do something or be somebody because we are not satisfied with ourselves or with the state of the world. We have a deep desire to relieve suffering. You may say that you need to run because what you are running toward is worthwhile, but running toward what you think is good is *still* running—you will still suffer.

"Aimlessness" means not running after anything anymore. It means not putting an object in front of you and continually reaching for it. Whether that object is fame, profit, or sensual pleasure, whether it's social justice or even enlightenment, as long as we are attached to seeking it, we will never experience freedom from suffering. The teaching of aimlessness is a deep and wonderful teaching.

OUR TRUE DESIRE

If we are able to quiet the cravings within us, we see that our true desire is not wealth or fame but happiness. Because we want happiness, we search for power outside of ourselves. But as long as we seek power and happiness in fame, money, and sex, we will not find it. Only by coming back to ourselves and purifying our minds can we experience true, lasting happiness.

THE ART OF STOPPING

We have to learn the art of stopping: stopping our thinking, our habit energies, our forgetfulness, and the strong emotions that rule us. When an emotion rushes through us like a storm, we have no peace. We turn on the TV and then we turn it off. We pick up a book and then we put it down. How can we stop this state of agitation? How can we stop our fear, despair, anger, and craving?

We can stop by practicing mindful breathing, mindful walking, and deep looking in order to understand. When we are mindful, when we touch the present moment deeply, the fruits we reap are always understanding, acceptance, love, and the desire to relieve suffering and bring joy.

HABIT ENERGIES, VOLITION, AND MINDFULNESS

Our habit energies are often stronger than our deepest dreams. We say and do things we don't want to and afterward we regret it. We make ourselves and others suffer, and we do a lot of damage, over and over again. Why? Because our habit energies are driving us.

We need the energy of mindfulness to recognize and be present with our habit energy in order to stop this course of destruction. With mindfulness, we have the capacity to recognize the habit energy every time it manifests. "Hello, my little habit energy, I know you are there!" If we just smile to it, it will lose much of its strength. Mindfulness is the energy that allows us to recognize our habits and prevent them from controlling us.

STOPPING, UNDERSTANDING

When we learn to stop, we begin to look
deeply, and when we look deeply, we
understand. The fruit of looking deeply is
understanding the many causes and conditions
that have brought about our current situation.
With this kind of insight, we know what to
do and what not to do to take better care of
ourselves—individually and collectively.

SPIRITUAL SUPPORT

Sometimes your intellect tells you that it's dangerous to embrace this or that object of desire. You know that you'll suffer, but you can't resist and do it anyway. Without a wise friend, without a spiritual community that can protect and help you, you often do such things in spite of your better judgment.

A GOOD FRIEND

A good spiritual friend is someone who can help us uncover our deepest desire. That person can inspire us to touch the seed of deep aspiration, and we become motivated to find out what we really want—not just on the surface but deep down.

THE BELOVED COMMUNITY

From the first moment I met the Reverend Martin Luther King Jr., I knew I was in the presence of a holy person. Not just his good work but his very being was a source of great inspiration for me. Dr. King and I agreed that without a happy, harmonious community, we cannot go very far—we cannot realize our dream. After he was assassinated, I made a deep vow to continue building what he called "the beloved community."

NOT AN INDIVIDUAL MATTER

The Buddha urged us to practice mindful living, to practice transformation and healing, as a community. When the community embodies the spirit of the Dharma, it can produce collective insight and lasting social change.

THE LIVING DHARMA

What is the Dharma? There is the spoken Dharma, the spoken teachings of the Buddha, and there is the written Dharma that we can find in books. But the best kind of Dharma is the living Dharma. When you practice mindful breathing, mindful walking, mindful sitting, you bring peace to yourself, you get understanding and compassion, and you radiate peace. That is the living Dharma. If we practice, we can all embody and radiate the living Dharma.

LIVING IN HARMONY AND AWARENESS

In Buddhism, a practice community is called a *sangha*. Any group of people can practice as a sangha, as a community that is determined to live in harmony and awareness. All we have to do is commit ourselves to going together in the direction of peace, joy, and freedom. Together, we benefit from each other's strengths and learn from each other's weaknesses.

A sangha is a family, a spiritual family connected by the practices of mindfulness, concentration, and insight. A sangha does not have to be Buddhist, as long as it is a community that walks the path of liberation together. To fulfill this goal, we need concrete practices; we need the collective insight and wisdom to guide and support us.

MY TRUTH

Here's a truth I live each day, proof that my dream is being realized: I live in a community of several hundred monks and nuns from many different countries, yet everyone can accept, forgive, and support each other. Everyone contributes to our shared well-being, and no one chases their own individual happiness because they know there's no such thing. We learn to cultivate togetherness and true friendship, helping each other transform our suffering and find joy in our daily lives. No one tries to be the boss. We live like bees of the same hive, working for our collective happiness.

MAKING THE PRACTICE EASY AND NATURAL

Joining or creating a like-minded community is very helpful for our practice. When we practice together as a community, our practice of mindfulness becomes more joyful, more relaxed, and steadier. We are bells of mindfulness for each other, supporting and reminding each other along the path of practice. With the support of the community, we can cultivate peace and joy in ourselves, which we can then offer to those around us.

The encouragement and support of a sangha, a community of practice, can help us enormously. When we practice together, mindfulness becomes easy and natural.

SPIRITUAL AND SOCIAL REALMS

Each person practicing mindfulness in a
community becomes a kind of social worker
in the broadest sense of the word. When you
help people taste the joy of spiritual practice,
you are doing social work. The spiritual and
the social realms are not separated. Whatever
you can do as a community in the spiritual
realm will benefit the social realm deeply
and directly.

A COMMUNITY OF RESISTANCE

A sangha is also a community of resistance, resisting the speed, violence, and unwholesome ways of living that are prevalent in our society. A good sangha can lead us in the direction of harmony and awareness. It can help us touch the seed of awakening within our heart so that we will have the courage to act.

THE POWER OF ACTION

Every moment that we're alive in this body, in this human manifestation, we're emitting energy. This energy can be transformed but it can't die; it remains in the world forever. The Sanskrit word for this is *karma*, which simply means "action." Karma is the triple action of our body, speech, and mind.

Karma is very powerful. The thoughts and feelings we send out into the world have a powerful effect. We have to recognize the power of our karma and make a firm determination to be mindful of our thoughts, speech, and actions in order to heal ourselves and the earth.

ACTION IS BASED ON NONACTION

The quality of being determines the quality of doing. An action must be based on nonaction. We usually say: "Don't just sit there: do something." But we have to reverse that statement to say: "Don't just do something: sit there," so we can cultivate the energy that makes peace, understanding, and compassion possible.

RIGHT THOUGHT, SPEECH, AND ACTION

Thought and speech are forms of action. Thoughts have an immediate effect on our health and on the health of the world. A positive thought will bring us physical and mental health, and it will help the world to heal itself. This is Right Thinking.

Right Speech inspires understanding, joy, hope, and togetherness. Speaking words that express kindness and compassion make us feel better in body and mind; they bring healing and transformation to ourselves, others, and the world.

Right Action refers to our physical actions. When we perform a physical action that has the power to protect, save, support, or bring relief, that action brings healing to us and to the world right away.

CLEAR CRITERION FOR RIGHT ACTION

Right or wrong action can be determined by using the single criterion of suffering or non-suffering. Whatever causes suffering in the present or the future, for ourselves and people around us, is the wrong thing to do. What brings well-being in the present and the future is the right thing. The criterion is clear.

COLLECTIVE KARMA

For the healing of our world, we need to create a community of practice. The energy of our thoughts, speech, and actions is infinitely more powerful when we join together with others. When we come together as a group, with a common purpose and commitment to mindful action, we produce an energy of collective concentration far superior to our own individual concentration.

If we practice mindful sitting, walking, speaking, and listening together as a group, the energy we create is amplified. Everyone can receive nourishment and healing, and this collective energy can lead to collective insight.

KEEPING YOUR ASPIRATION ALIVE

We have to organize our lives in such a way that we can continue to get the nourishment and healing that we need. The solution is in your community. If you build a community that practices together as a sangha, you receive the collective energy of support. When you begin to feel exhausted by your efforts, others in your community are there to help with the work; you can take time to restore yourself so that you can continue serving your deep aspiration.

YOUR OWN WORK OF ART

Each of us has to sit down and look deeply to see what we can be, what we can do today to help relieve the suffering around us, to help reduce stress, and to bring about more joy and happiness. We can do this by ourselves or with a group of people, with our colleagues or with our family. There is so much suffering in the world but, at the same time, there is also the potential for so much joy. By living your life with awareness, producing your own work of art, you can contribute to the work of collective awakening.

GENERATING JOY

"Breathing in, I bring in a pleasant feeling, a feeling of joy." This is not mere imagination or wishful thinking. It's possible to generate these feelings with mindfulness. Breathing in mindfully, you may get the insight that so many conditions of happiness are available right this minute. Your feet are strong, your eyes are still in good condition, your ears can hear all kinds of sounds, and you can enjoy walking. Walking meditation becomes a pleasure, a delight. When you touch the conditions of happiness with mindfulness, joy is born naturally—the joy of being alive, the joy to heal, to nourish, to release tension, and the joy of practicing with others. We should be able to bring in a feeling of joy anytime we want.

NOURISHING THE MIND OF LOVE

It's because of love that we practice. We're not just trying to run away from suffering; we want more than that. We want to transform our own suffering and be free in order to help many other people transform their suffering. The mind of love is a powerful source of energy we should keep alive. So nourishing the mind of love, preserving bodhicitta, is a very important practice.

SANGHA ENCOURAGES BODHICITTA

One of the most important ways to nourish and protect our bodhicitta is to find a good sangha. If you have a sangha that is joyful, animated by the desire to practice and help, you will mature as a bodhisattva.

In a good and healthy sangha, there is encouragement for our bodhicitta. Your sangha is the soil, and you are the seed. No matter how vigorous the seed is, if the soil does not provide nourishment, the seed will die. A good sangha is crucial for keeping our bodhicitta alive.

BREAKING THE BARRIER OF INDIVIDUALISM

A bodhisattva is a living being animated by the strong desire to help awaken other people, relieve their suffering, and bring them happiness. An authentic bodhisattva embodies two elements: the great aspiration to liberate all beings and the wisdom of nondiscrimination.

The Buddha teaches us that there is no distinction between the one who saves and the living beings who are saved. This is a wonderful lesson: we don't take care of others—other people, animals, plants—out of any moral righteousness but because there's no distinction between us. The wisdom of nondiscrimination breaks the barrier of individualism.

When we can see there is no difference between self and other, then we're a bodhisattva, a fully awakened person.

THE EYES OF TOGETHERNESS

We must learn to look with the eyes of togetherness rather than each looking out for ourselves. We must learn to love in the spirit of nondiscrimination, without seeing ourselves as superior, inferior, or equal to others, and recognize the truth that we and others are *not two*. With the eyes of nondiscrimination, true humanism and kinship become possible.

THE GLOBAL COMMUNITY

The ancient saying "peoples of the four oceans are brothers" is not just a dream. With the insight of nondiscrimination, we recognize that the peace, safety, and prosperity of other nations is our own peace, safety, and prosperity. We do not want to close our doors and lock ourselves within our own borders but open our doors so that everyone can see that we too are a member of the global community. This is true togetherness.

THE POWER TO BRING RELIEF

When we're free, we can do so many things to help our people, our community. It's possible to live simply and happily. When we transform ourselves into a bodhisattva, a great being, we generate a lot of power. It's not the power of fame or wealth. It's the kind of power that helps us to be free and bring relief to many people.

THE FIVE MINDFULNESS TRAININGS: A SOURCE OF ENERGY

The Five Mindfulness Trainings are the substance of a bodhisattva.* By living our lives according to the Five Mindfulness Trainings, we become bodhisattvas and we live not only for ourselves, but for the well-being of others; our life serves as a source of energy for their happiness.

When we practice the Five Mindfulness Trainings, we become bodhisattvas helping to create harmony, protect the environment, safeguard peace, and cultivate connection. If we know how to apply the Five Mindfulness Trainings, individually and collectively, then peace on earth will become a reality.

---

* A North Star for Dreamers," the next part of this book starting on page 105, introduces all five trainings for deeper reflection.

A PATH FOR HUMANITY

From the time of his first teaching delivered to his first disciples, the Buddha was very clear and practical about how we can transform our difficulties, both individually and collectively. He focused on how we put the teachings into practice in our everyday lives. That is ethics.

It is important for us not to focus on ethics in the abstract. Our basic practice is generating the energy of mindfulness, concentration, and insight. These three energies are the foundation of all Buddhist practice and Buddhist ethics.

With the energy of mindfulness, concentration, and insight, you can build a path for humanity—a path of peace and happiness, a path of transformation and healing.

THE EFFECT OF ONE PERSON'S DREAM

The desire to grow our understanding and compassion and to help the world is a wonderful energy that gives our lives genuine purpose. Many great teachers before us—Jesus, Buddha, Mohammed, and Moses—also had this aspiration. Today we experience the same profound dream as they did: to embody peace, relieve suffering, and help people. We have seen that one person can bring liberation and healing to thousands, even millions of people. Each one of us, whether a factory worker, a politician, a businessperson, or an entertainer, carries the seed of bodhicitta. But it is important to remember that, to realize this deep dream, we must first take care of ourselves.

A NORTH STAR
FOR DREAMERS

THE FIVE MINDFULNESS TRAININGS

The Five Mindfulness Trainings are concrete practices of compassion and understanding for our daily lives. They are nonsectarian and their nature is universal; they are not commandments, and they are offered without dogma or religion. Anyone at any time can decide to live by the Five Mindfulness Trainings, which, although rooted in traditional Buddhist ethics, are practices we can all adopt regardless of faith. When we practice the Five Mindfulness Trainings, we become bodhisattvas helping to create harmony, protect the environment, safeguard peace, and cultivate togetherness. With the Five Mindfulness Trainings in our hearts, we are already on the path of transformation and healing.

Studying and practicing the mindfulness trainings can help us understand the true nature of interbeing—we cannot be by ourselves alone; we can only inter-be with everyone and everything else. To practice these trainings is to become aware of what is going on in our bodies, our minds, and the world. With awareness, we can live our lives happily, fully present in each moment we are alive, intelligently seeking solutions to the problems we face, and working for peace in small and large ways.

It should be a joy, not a chore, to live according to the Five Mindfulness Trainings. We feel lucky to be able to live in a way that makes our planet's future a real possibility. If, with your practice of the Five Mindfulness Trainings, you feel that your understanding, loving kindness, and compassion have increased, then you can share your practice with others. In that way, we can realize our dream and make the world a better place.

THE FIRST
MINDFULNESS TRAINING:
REVERENCE FOR LIFE

Aware of the suffering caused by the destruction of life, I am committed to cultivating the insight of interbeing and compassion and learning ways to protect the lives of people, animals, plants, and minerals. I am determined not to kill, not to let others kill, and not to support any act of killing in the world, in my thinking, or in my way of life. Seeing that harmful actions arise from anger, fear, greed, and intolerance, which in turn come from dualistic and discriminative thinking, I will cultivate openness, nondiscrimination, and nonattachment to views in order to transform violence, fanaticism, and dogmatism in myself and in the world.

THE SECOND
MINDFULNESS TRAINING:
TRUE HAPPINESS

Aware of the suffering caused by exploitation,
social injustice, stealing, and oppression, I am
committed to practicing generosity in my thinking, speaking, and acting. I am determined
not to steal and not to possess anything that
should belong to others; and I will share my
time, energy, and material resources with those
who are in need. I will practice looking deeply
to see that the happiness and suffering of others are not separate from my own happiness
and suffering; that true happiness is not possible without understanding and compassion;
and that running after wealth, fame, power
and sensual pleasures can bring much suffering and despair. I am aware that happiness

depends on my mental attitude and not on external conditions, and that I can live happily in the present moment simply by remembering that I already have more than enough conditions to be happy. I am committed to practicing Right Livelihood so that I can help reduce the suffering of living beings on Earth and stop contributing to climate change.

THE THIRD
MINDFULNESS TRAINING:
TRUE LOVE

Aware of the suffering caused by sexual misconduct, I am committed to cultivating respon-
sibility and learning ways to protect the safety
and integrity of individuals, couples, families,
and society. Knowing that sexual desire is not
love, and that sexual activity motivated by
craving always harms myself as well as others, I am determined not to engage in sexual
relations without mutual consent, true love,
and a deep, long-term commitment. I resolve
to find spiritual support for the integrity of my
relationship from family members, friends, and
sangha with whom there is support and trust.
I will do everything in my power to protect
children from sexual abuse and to prevent

couples and families from being broken by sexual misconduct. Seeing that body and mind are interrelated, I am committed to learn appropriate ways to take care of my sexual energy and to cultivate the four basic elements of true love—loving kindness, compassion, joy, and inclusiveness—for the greater happiness of myself and others. Recognizing the diversity of human experience, I am committed not to discriminate against any form of gender identity or sexual orientation. Practicing true love, we know that we will continue beautifully into the future.

THE FOURTH MINDFULNESS TRAINING: LOVING SPEECH AND DEEP LISTENING

Aware of the suffering caused by unmindful speech and the inability to listen to others, I am committed to cultivating loving speech and compassionate listening in order to relieve suffering and to promote reconciliation and peace in myself and among other people, ethnic and religious groups, and nations. Knowing that words can create happiness or suffering, I am committed to speaking truthfully using words that inspire confidence, joy, and hope. When anger is manifesting in me, I am determined not to speak. I will practice mindful breathing and walking in order to recognize and to look deeply into my anger. I know that the roots of anger can be found in my wrong perceptions and lack of understanding of the suffering in myself and in the other person. I will speak and listen in a way that can help myself and the other person to transform suffering and see the way out of difficult situations. I am determined not to spread news that I do not know to be certain and not to utter words that can cause division or discord. I will practice Right Diligence to nourish my capacity for understanding, love, joy, and inclusiveness, and gradually transform anger, violence, and fear that lie deep in my consciousness.

THE FIFTH
MINDFULNESS TRAINING:
NOURISHMENT AND HEALING

Aware of the suffering caused by unmindful consumption, I am committed to cultivating good health, both physical and mental, for myself, my family, and my society by practicing mindful eating, drinking, and consuming. I will practice looking deeply into how I consume the Four Kinds of Nutriments, namely edible foods, sense impressions, volition, and consciousness. I am determined not to gamble or use alcohol, drugs, or any other products which contain toxins, such as certain websites, electronic games, TV programs, films, magazines, books, and conversations. I will practice coming back to the present moment to be in touch with the refreshing, healing and nourishing elements in me and around me, not letting regrets and sorrow drag me back into the past nor letting anxieties, fear, or craving pull me out of the present moment. I am determined not to try to cover up loneliness, anxiety, or other suffering by losing myself in consumption. I will contemplate interbeing and consume in a way that preserves peace, joy, and well-being in my body and consciousness, and in the collective body and consciousness of my family, my society, and the earth.

Monastics and visitors practice the art of mindful living in the tradition of Thich Nhat Hanh at our mindfulness practice centers around the world. To reach any of these communities, or for information about how individuals, couples, and families can join in a retreat, please contact:

Plum Village
33580 Dieulivol, France
plumvillage.org

Blue Cliff Monastery
Pine Bush, NY 12566, USA
bluecliffmonastery.org

**European Institute of
Applied Buddhism**
D-51545 Waldbröl, Germany
eiab.eu

Healing Spring Monastery
77510 Verdelot,
France
healingspringmonastery.org

**Asian Institute of
Applied Buddhism**
Ngong Ping, Lantau Island
Hong Kong
pvfhk.org

Mountain Spring Monastery
Bilpin, Victoria 2758
Australia
mountainspringmonastery.org

Magnolia Grove Monastery
Batesville, MS 38606, USA
magnoliagrovemonastery.org

Deer Park Monastery
Escondido, CA 92026, USA
deerparkmonastery.org

Thailand Plum Village
Nakhon Ratchasima
30130 Thailand
thaiplumvillage.org

Maison de l'Inspir
77510 Villeneuve-sur-Bellot
France
maisondelinspir.org

**Nhap Luu-Stream
Entering Monastery**
Porcupine Ridge, Victoria 3461
Australia
nhapluu.org

Further Resources

For information about our international community, visit: plumvillage.org

To find an online sangha, visit: plumline.org

For more practices and resources, download the Plum Village app: plumvillage.app

THICH NHAT HANH FOUNDATION

planting seeds of Compassion

THE THICH NHAT HANH FOUNDATION works to
continue the mindful teachings and practice of Zen
Master Thich Nhat Hanh, in order to foster peace and
transform suffering in all people, animals, plants, and
our planet. Through donations to the Foundation,
thousands of generous supporters ensure the continu-
ation of Plum Village practice centers and monastics
around the world, bring transformative practices to
those who otherwise would not be able to access
them, support local mindfulness initiatives, and bring
humanitarian relief to communities in crisis in Vietnam.

By becoming a supporter, you join many others
who want to learn and share these life-changing
practices of mindfulness, loving speech, deep listening, and compassion for oneself, each other, and
the planet.

For more information on how you can help support
mindfulness around the world, or to subscribe to the
Foundation's monthly newsletter with teachings,
news, and global retreats, visit **tnhf.org**.